I0418058

Edutainment Nite Publishing, LLC
Third Edition, 2024
BFAP Icons
Second Printing, 2014
Anotha Planetary Level Productions
First Printing, 1997

DEDICATED

To all my people in the everyday struggle that enjoys public transportation as much as I do and to all the people that didn't call the police on me.

BFAP NSIGHTINGS @ DA BUS STOP

BFAP nSIGHTINGS @ da Bus Stop

A Poetry Collection
1995–1997

M.C. MoHagani Magnetek

Edutainment Nite Publishing, LLC

CONTENTS

EARLY WISDOM

Optimism shrouds illusion when at the vortex
on the verge of finding a solution
To counteract systematic pressures
Everyday is filled with numerous
possibilities and great measures
Just to attain the basic necessities
for longevity and duration
Patience and determination
almost always resembles an occupation

Day breaks once more as the earth rest til noon
If the game show ever ends, it will be too soon
A young woman gifted and black

All the experiences in the world, but still lack
Stability and dominion in her inner space
Success surrounds her lips for the after taste
Clarity and direction are gifts from the Gods
To aid her travels against all odds
Desperately trying to catch a note
To finish the melody her ancestors wrote

The reality is, she is a piece of human
trying to become a whole
In the late hours stranded in the cold
The truth is the only story that remains to be told
Long after the last word in the book is written
Purgatives and cleansers are only for the bitten
Sufficing at the thought of another attack

Lorraine Hansberry,
it sure is a battle to be young, gifted and black.

SOMETIME AGO ON METRO

Last nite
I was yelling on the bus.
Man, I was preaching.
I was schoolin' my people
Bout Africa ad being African
Up and down the aisle
Yo Sista! Yo Brotha!
Let's get together
and build a nation,
a nation of liberated Africans
Let's construct study groups
to read and study our
foundations,
contributions
and struggles.
The whole time
the bus is cruising.
Black people getting,
Black people getting off.

ANSWERS IN THE FORM OF QUESTIONS

Does it begin with the swing of Satchamo
Over a delicate evening and dim lights?

Does it begin with a whisper on a jazzy morning
Filled with numerous possibilities?

Does it begin with the prologue of that favorite
lesson or novel?

Does it begin in the early stages
of spirit transformation
into a splendid dream?

Does it begin with the pleasant feeling of comfort
Surrounded by the echoes
of trees and the ruffles of animals?

Does it begin at all?

MAN, SPIRITS DON'T CHASE

Spirits be calling, spirits be calling
If you listen you can hear them calling
Wake up child, you got work to do
There's a plan, a destiny, a design
Specifically for you

No more running, no more
Hiding from the path has always been
before you even had the choice to realize
They put in place the persistence
and determination in your eyes
Yet unborn and children live for elders
and ancestors who have
completed their work on this plane
Until you do right by them
They will be calling your name

All of life's many aspects can be utilized
as attributes for those in pursuit of

life, liberty and happiness and nothing else
The answers were written
on the ancient temples, "Know Thyself"

Spirits be calling, spirits be calling
If you listen you can hear them calling
Wake up child
and see them reaching for you
trying to save you from
false reality, all that is not true
Don't give up
even when you're down and out
The spirits will whisper and shout
And throw you a lifesaver
to keep you from drowning   ·
They know how the pressure
keeps on pounding and pounding
In your eclectic spirit
Pay attention and you should hear it
True enough some will fall
to the waste side
Only cuz when the spirits were calling
they run and hide
Running and hiding from help

Only fools
who don't have a concept of self
Will run from blessings words of
wisdom, knowledge and other lessons

ON SEEING A LIL BROTHA

Mama, ain't but 19 with three babies
One she calls man, the other son
and the last is yet unborn
A black family can't live but only survive
In a day to day slot machine
Wishing that all the copper
and silver would become green
Just long enough for
the baby's birthday party
And give him a taste of something
other than Bacardi
That will only leave him
with a pocket full of worries
And he will still be intoxicated
In the meantime
Mom is urging dad to get educated
While mom and dad are trying
to make ends meet
He will suffice off his bread and meat

DAILY TRAVELS

This morning on the limo
my uncle was the driver
A ride, 2-Day pass
being with kinfolk
couldn't have been much liver
The situation led me to
the female root worker from Uganda
Such an experience makes way
for many things to ponder
The spoken word led me to
brotha Mussa's shop
Engaged in vibing with my brethren
carrying-on and what-not
Exchange currency for some
essence oils and licorice root
Many destinations in limited time
I must be in hot pursuit
A sister at project row consults
me on grooming my locs
I agreed to advertise her
natural hair workshops

Share love with my
Sista in the struggle over education
Received a five dollar
credit for participation
In the movement
through cooperative economics
and concern
For the love of my people
I must learn
Lessons about
rivalries, informants, political prisoners
not set free
Every bit of today's experiences
Adds a little
more depth and understanding to me

CANDLELIGHT

A storm outside of Big Mama's house
Can't see a thing but each other
Only when we come close together
Conjuring up good times
Hoping they will come again
In the shadows of bad weather
The more experience teacher helps
The less experience student to grow
She mixes
all the nutrients and lessons of life
in a pot of gumbo
Sauna brings sweat like teardrops
to roll down my face
Allowing imagination to experience
another place
Where sleep joins in on our conversation.
Candlelight becomes
the most precious of God's creation

MY MOTHER AFRICA

You know who's been on my mind all day
My mother, Africa
She is sooooo sweet, lemme tell you
She woke me up this morning by
stretching out her arms and anointing Bob Marley
Oh the sound of spiritual revolution
Really conjures up something inside of me!
Then she took her other arm
and reached out for the orange tree
She picked the juiciest of the juiciest
Orange the tree had to offer and gently
Squeezed luscious drops on the end of my tongue
Although we have long distance relationship
cuz I was taken from her at birth
She still loves me the same
Every morning
I hear her calling my name

My mother Africa is sumpthin' else
About two years ago when I felt alone and
Confused, she started teaching me lessons

About self by sending me on a journey
She took me to the river and
baptized me in her womb
She started twisting and turning the wool on
My head until it made these spirals
reaching for the sun
And then falling to the earth
She told me they are solar roots
I guess it's cuz of the sun-earth thing
This journey my mother Africa sent me
on has me in spirals
Although we have a long distance relationship
Cuz I was taken from her at birth
She still loves me the same
Everyday at midday
I hear her calling my name

My mother Africa is sumpthin' else!
She calls me home to tell me great stories
She told me how
great my great-great grandparents were
Some stories are happy, and some are sad
Like how I was taken from her womb and
Became captive on other islands and continents
She always tells me that story so
I won't forget
She teaches me how to work with
my sistas and brothas
How to pay homage to the ancestors.

My mother Africa is the best
Cuz of my love for her, I will fight anybody
who talks bad about her or try to harm her!

To me every day is
Mother Africa's Day
cuz every time
She calls my name
I go running home

27 MINUTES TO 12

27 minutes to 12
and she's pregnant
Standing at the bus stop
on the way to the clinic
3 children before Norplant and it's her
Husband's 1st... possessing
excitement, anxiety and insecurity
About the reality
that she's about to have another
Baby 27 minutes to 12
She awaits her high-class limousine
to go to the clinic
Before getting on she tosses away
the last of her cancer stick.

OBSERVATION OF THE 3RD ROCK FROM THE SUN

somehow the sky touches the earth
or maybe the earth touches the sky.
some trees are tall and some are short
melodies linger in the air long
after the bird sang the last note.
above all of this is the sun, with rays on
under, around and through everything.
eye see why people worship god.

OVERLOOKING CITY STREETS

Cars passing by with intended destinations
Sirens of pigs signal departure
from their stations into a hot climate
Meanwhile rebels run amuck on the streets
Begging for a metamorphosis, just a little
Bit of metamorphosis to get a fix
Through sonic waves crickets
carry on good conversation
The conversations must be deep
cause they talk all night
Gill-Scott Heron adds
a touch of spice to the mood
He offers the intellect
a little something to soothe
Into the next plateau with a perfect
Transition and easy flow

Yellow light, red light, green

Directs thaNOMAD on her travels
Last night's rain has left its memory on the
Earth and is still leaping from the tree leaves
Headlights, streetlights, porch lights
Makes the evening even a little clearer
But do not make up for the depths of
Blackness bestowed on the moon's domain
Urban rhythms are dancing on the crickets'
Conversations in exchange for time
Red lights, green lights, yellow

No children to be found only the wino
Conquers the street with a forty-ounce
and forty million stories
The whole time still trying to get a
metamorphosis in the middle of nowhere
But stuck in the chambers of
Headlights, streetlights porch lights
This time the ambulance is racing
Blasting lyrics for the suffering
on a mission to save them
The trees come alive and juba down
While the wind takes the role as the DJ

Green light, yellow light red

WHAT TO DO IN PASSING

Step by step we come closer together,
from a distance he was a blare.
The closer we come, the longer I stare.
Klink-Klink the wheels of the basket
tap dance on the asphalt.
He was not alone in the middle of the air
where his essence was caught.
What appears to be
a homeless bag man
and a young fool.
We make eye contact,
nod our head and say,
"What's going on?"
Taking heed in the blacks in passing rule.

JUST FOR AESTHETICS

a simple stroll through the Tré
to admire the sweet nectar of the day
while meditating on some funky vibrations
sitting at the feet of elders during libations
dance with some ancestors over drums
or chase some homies with water guns
gaze at a big-haired blond pace the streets
cherish the victories and learn from defeats
set in motion a nice groove with my lady
take her for dinner and a movie on payday
read a book in the park before sunset
or put my feet in the lake to get a little wet
after the good movie, read the credits
all for some simple just aesthetics.

maybe some HipHop for the soul
and reminisce on the days of old
whether beatboxing or break dancing
everything we got on, it was about enhancing
adding the icing on the cake
being with kinfolks looking for cookies to bake

to accompany a Friday night rental movie
reading Ellison's
The Invisible Man or black history
maybe incense and jazz on the rise with the sun
or playing like children, having a child's kind of fun
take a nap underneath an oak tree for shade
on an imaginary quest for some sacred jade
picking fresh flowers for that significant other
feeling the presence of love from your mother
or maybe some dawn or dusk calisthenics
all for some simple just aesthetics.

get as close but not wet by the evening rain
moving swiftly from Monk to Coltrane
or maybe a pizza by candlelight
along with Mother Earth for the flight
creating patterns on a canvas for expression
and searching for depth in mental session
a Troubled Man by Marvin Gaye sounds nice
listening to the elders, taking heed in their advice
watching some Saturday morning cartoons
or sleeping in way past noon
going to church in your Sunday best
or walking to anywhere, thanking God to blessed
some days anywhere it can be so majestic
all for some simple just aesthetics.

WAITING FOR MY LIMOUSINE

Waiting there.
Where here stops the bus.
No one is here or there.
Just Me Myself and I. Just Us.
Sumpthin' makes Us wanna holla.
Damn, We ain't gots no dollar.
Just some change
We must unite piece by piece.
We had to do some digging cuz
Our low income doesn't seem to cease
Getting lower and lower.
By now the limo moves closer much slower.
In front of Us (that's Me Myself and I)
it comes to a halt.
We step onto the limo and off the asphalt.
It takes a while for the machine to count
Our change.
To the back of the bus
with people looking at Us all strange.

KOZMIC

Life is a spindle of many circles
Composed of horizontals and verticals
Blessings a dime a dozen every other day
Tough hours require concrete floors to lay
Place tension on tense areas of the temple
If only life was self-explanatory
or at least that simple
Maybe the hitchhiker can have a bus token
And the children
will heed the words that are spoken
The thinker uses a diary to reflect
thoughts and even desires
About the external and internal fires
Someone once said
that nobody knows where to find
Revolution by the book
When push comes to shove
the street signs tell you where to look
All truth is found in the last place sought
Which is inside with intuitive thought

ELEMENTAL SENSES

I guess poetry calls
the mood and brings the day into being
Without a doubt
it is the blind man
that is the only one seeing
Most clearly all the images of motion

Without a doubt
it is the deaf woman
that hears all the commotion
That the queen raises trying
to remember her essential vibe
Without a doubt
it is the mute child
that has no secrets to hide

A troubled man
carries many woes in his bag of cans
Escaping the summer's heat by
wiping his brow with his hands
His story is heard and understood by the wino

Whose disillusion, confusion and sorrow
Is the sum of what he actually know
About caged birds in stormy weathers
Fighting fiercely to shed more feathers
Crazy isn't it
how life resembles the playground
Children laugh, play and go round and round
Until they all fall down
Resting on the earth alone with only sound

LADY ELEGANCE GRACE

Words tap dance on my windowsill
So I let her in to see all that I conceal
And got me trapped and lost
in this world of romance
Where my thoughts and desires enhance

I am a Lady.

And oh' how loved the dance
Last night, an angel led me
center stage for my chance

My name is Elegance.

I spent all of my time on the dance floor
Hands outlined shadows as eyes explore
There's no reason to chase the love of Grace

Yesterday prophesized that today

I will know the love
That tomorrow is always speaking of
I became the only queen to share inner space
That why I call myself, Lady Elegance Grace.

STOP AT THE CROSSROADS

"On the corner many things happen,
Many things are always happening."

It was on the corner
I sat with some cat watching the cars go by
Some cars were lemons; some cats were high

On the corner
on a hot summer day
Me and the other cats
were rappin' as time gave way

Yesterday on the corner
some child got shot
Drive-by (not my reality)
stray bullet, he was dead on the spot

On the corner
last night I met a gal with style

Man, I was all caught up
in those pretty legs and that sexy smile

This morning on the corner
some car in a car honked at me
Turned out to be a pig
that thought I was his "G"
(I had no I.D.)

On the corner at lunchtime...
"Hey, Dread!
Can you spare a brotha a dime?
That's all I need to get sumpthin' to eat.
I should have a legit hustle by the end of the week."

Just a minute ago on the corner
two cats started scrapping
I had to leave then,
cuz too much was happening

SENTENCE FRAGMENTS & COMPLETE THOUGHTS

have you ever looked down the very ground you walk on and contemplated the aspect of life through a song you heard the other morning or maybe just a minute ago; the thought of melodies are transported through the flow of one spirit to the next, simple answers were once complex questions with beginnings and no endings; on the road you have shun many enemies and gained many friends; some stranger than the stranger who just happens to be in the eye scope of the ranger, but the focus is narrowed and fixed on a place not designated by the second or the hour, but somewhere in infinity is the power of inner space and outer mind from start to finish is the line, but it doesn't stand alone; the spirit guarded the energy, spirit answers the wish of an ounce of something good passing on from your last thought and the place you stood.

RAIN, RAIN DON'T GO AWAY

On a rainy day
I sit down
and burn incense
at the bus stop
While waiting to be
transported from
the A to the B dot
The shelter becomes
consumed by the sweet
smell of incense
diffusing with the rain
I'm in a relax
state of emotions
between joy and pain
I imagine
what it would be like
to create the same
Atmosphere for
the other passengers

I'll be offering
heart filled blessings
to complete strangers
Children play
rain, rain go away
Come back another day
With whispers in prayer
I say,
"All praise is due
onto the creator
for today's vibration."
I watch the water
evaporate from the earth
as if the land is giving birth
To the sky
only for it to rain again

WHAT FOLKS DO FOR MONEY

It's 10 O'clock at night
and I'm meditating at the bus stop
The hooker on the corner next to me
is trying to shake the spot
Integrating the streetlight scene
Exchanging conjured passion for some green
Money that belongs to the white cats
on the other side of town
Got the sista selling private personal parts
after the knockdown
It reminds me of the other morning
when two kids about fifteen asked me
tha Being From Anotha Planet
if I saw some dope fiends
Youngbloods trying to make a buck
Selling crack like the sista sell her stuff
Whoever said a Pan-African revolution
 is irrelevant didn't see what I saw
or they would know it is absolutely evident

DESTINATION SELF

Before I lay me down to sleep
I pray to the lord my soul shall keep
As I make my way into this spiritual bliss
Leaving this world I'm on an exodus

Out of day and into night
Searching
while running from the ultraviolet light
Cruise control and a staying calm
Peace on earth is hard to find for some

For me it comes easy
I just close my eyes and let becoming be
Missions are for Jesuit priest
The distance
between me and the creator must be the least

From here to there, the closest to none
Virtues I attain and fetters I shun
Transmigration through purification
Returning to my planet is my destination.

About the Author

M.C. MoHagani Magnetek (pronounced emcee mahogany magnetic), is the proud mom of Sade Adamu. She's an amazing multi-talented individual with bachelor's degrees in Anthropology and English, plus an MFA in Creative Writing and Literary Arts. Right now, she's diving into her Ph.D. studies in Historical Archaeology, Museology, and Cultural Anthropology at the University of Alaska Fairbanks.

MoHagani is not just a student; she's a vibrant writer, poet, mistress of ceremonies, museum curator, and martial artist. She's also the creative force behind Edutainment Nite Publishing, where she serves as founder and publisher. As a Coast Guard veteran and passionate community organizer, MoHagani advocates for mental wellness and human rights. She's often celebrated as the undisputed people's champ because she truly believes in the healing power of poetry.

Currently, she's on a journey to get her life together while enjoying roller skating and practicing Kung Fu in Alaska with her lovely wife, Juanita. Frying fish is MoHagani's favorite pastime.